MERRILL Science

AUTHORS

Dr. Jay K. Hackett
University of Northern Colorado

Dr. Richard H. Moyer
University of Michigan-Dearborn

Dr. Donald K. Adams
University of Northern Colorado

Contributing Writer
Ann H. Sankey
Science Specialist
Educational Service District 121
Seattle, Washington

Reading Consultant
Barbara S. Pettegrew, Ph.D.
Director of the Reading/Study Center
Assistant Professor of Education
Otterbein College
Westerville, Ohio

Safety Consultant
Gary E. Downs, Ed.D.
Professor
Iowa State University
Ames, Iowa

Gifted and Mainstreaming Consultants
George Fichter
Educational Consultant
Programs for Gifted
Ohio Department of Education
Worthington, Ohio

Timothy E. Heron, Ph.D.
Professor
Department of Human Services, Education
The Ohio State University
Columbus, Ohio

Primary Levels Consultant
Maureen E. Allen
Science Resource Specialist
Irvine Unified School District
Irvine, California

Content Consultants
Robert T. Brown, M.D.
Associate Professor of Clinical Pediatrics
Director, Section for Adolescent Health
The Ohio State University/Children's Hospital
Columbus, Ohio

Henry D. Drew, Ph.D.
Chemist
U.S. FDA, Division of Drug Analysis
St. Louis, Missouri

Judith L. Doyle, Ph.D.
Physics Teacher
Newark High School
Newark, Ohio

Todd F. Holzman, M.D.
Child Psychiatrist
Harvard Community Health Plan
Wellesley, Massachusetts

Knut J. Norstog, Ph.D.
Research Associate
Fairchild Tropical Garden
Miami, Florida

James B. Phipps, Ph.D.
Professor, Geology/Oceanography
Grays Harbor College
Aberdeen, Washington

R. Robert Robbins, Ph.D.
Associate Professor of Astronomy
Astronomy Department, University of Texas
Austin, Texas

Sidney E. White, Ph.D.
Professor
Department of Geology & Mineralogy
The Ohio State University
Columbus, Ohio

ACKNOWLEDGEMENT

The authors are deeply indebted to the late Robert B. Sund for his inspiration and guidance in the early development of this series.

MERRILL
PUBLISHING COMPANY
A Bell & Howell Information Company
Toronto • London • Sydney

Merrill Science Program Components

Student Editions, K-6
Teacher Editions, K-6
Teacher Resource Books, K-6
  (Reproducible Masters)
Big Books, K-2
SkillBuilders: A Process & Problem Solving
  Skillbook, Student Editions, K-6
SkillBuilders: A Process & Problem Solving
  Skillbook, Teacher Editions, K-6

Poster Packets: Science in Your World, K-6
Color Transparencies, K-6
Activity Materials Kits, K-6
Activity Materials Management System
Awards Stickers
Science Words Software, 1-6
In-service Videotapes
Mr. Wizard Videos, 3-7
Science Fair Package

Dr. Jay K. Hackett is Professor of Earth Science Education at the University of Northern Colorado. He holds a B.S. in General Science, an M.N.S. in Physical Science, and an Ed.D. in Science Education with support in Earth Science. A resource teacher for elementary schools, he conducts numerous workshops and professional seminars. With over 20 years of teaching experience, he has taught and consulted on science programs across all levels and remains active in local, state, and national science professional organizations.

Dr. Richard H. Moyer is Professor of Science Education at the University of Michigan, Dearborn. He holds a B.S. in Chemistry and Physics Education, an M.S. in Curriculum and Instruction, and an Ed.D. in Science Education. With more than 19 years of teaching experience at all levels, he is currently involved in teacher training. He was the recipient of two Distinguished Faculty Awards. He conducts numerous workshops and in-service training programs for science teachers. Dr. Moyer is also the author of Merrill's *General Science* textbook.

Dr. Donald K. Adams is Professor of Education and Director, Education Field Experiences at the University of Northern Colorado. He holds a B.S. in Liberal Arts Social Science, an M.S. in Biological Science, and an Ed.D. in Science Education with support in Earth Science. In over 20 years of teaching, he has been instrumental in implementing personalized science and outdoor education programs and has served as a consultant to teacher preparation and science programs throughout the United States, Australia, and New Zealand.

Reviewers: Teachers and Administrators   **Virginia Ceruti,** Cleveland Elementary School, Norwood, MA; **Sister Teresa Fitzgerald,** CSJ, Office of Catholic Education, Brooklyn, NY; **JoAnn Hamm,** Danville Board of Education, Danville, KY; **Donna Jackson,** Hazel Avenue Elementary School, West Orange, NJ; **Norma Jones,** Austin Tracy School, Lucas, KY; **Barbara Kmetz,** Trumbull High School, Trumbull, CT; **Lee Dell McCarty,** United Methodist Publishing House, Nashville, TN; **Corinne Measelle,** Palm Beach County School Board, West Palm Beach, FL; **Waltina Mroczek,** Beachwood Elementary School, Beachwood, OH; **Linda Payne,** Whitesville Elementary School, Whitesville, KY; **Peggy Smith,** Special Education Resource Teacher, Fort Worth, TX; **Frank Stone,** Floranada Elementary School, Fort Lauderdale, FL; **Lana Tarlton,** Cook Elementary School, Austin, TX; **Dr. Rosa White,** Cutler Ridge Elementary School, Miami, FL

Cover Photo: Fox pup by Breck P. Kent
Series Editors: Karen S. Allen, Janet L. Helenthal; **Project Editor:** Linda Ashe McLaughlin; **Project Designer:** Joan Shaull; **Series Artist:** Dennis L. Smith; **Illustrators:** Nancy Heim, Kirchoff/Wohlberg, Inc., Jeanine S. Means, Publishers' Graphics, Inc.; **Photo Editor:** Barbara Buchholz; **Series Production Editor:** Joy E. Dickerson; **Project Production Editor:** Carole R. Hill

ISBN 0-675-03511-2

Published by

Merrill Publishing Co.
A Bell & Howell Information Company
Columbus, Ohio 43216

Copyright © 1989 by Merrill Publishing Co.
All rights reserved. No part of this book may be reproduced in any form, electronic or mechanical, including photocopy, recording, or any information storage or retrieval system, without permission in writing from the publisher.
Printed in the United States of America

Table of Contents

Chapter 1
You Find Out   2

Chapter 2
Animals   24

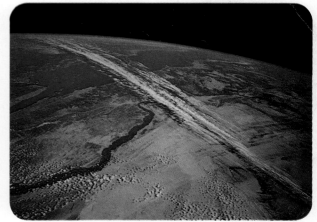

Chapter 5

All About You   90

Chapter 6

Earth and Space   112

Science in Your World

Do you like to explore?

Learning to explore is a part of science.

Science can help you answer questions.

Science will help you think of new questions.

What do you want to know about your world?

Science can help you learn.

Chapter 1

You Find Out

What is in your world?

How do you know?

Your Senses

You find out.

You use your senses.

What does he feel and smell?

How does it taste?

You see colors.

You see and feel shapes.

What do you know about these things?

What is in the box?

How can she guess?

Activity

What Is It?

1. Feel and smell each bag.
2. Shake each bag and listen.
3. What did you find out?
4. What do you see?

How Different?

Things are different.
How do you know?

Look at these animals.

How are they different?

Activity

Will It Float?

1. Find some things to try.
2. Guess which things float.
3. Make some groups.
4. Try each thing.

Solid or Liquid?

Some things are solid.

A solid has a shape.

Some things are liquid.

Liquids pour.

What shape is a liquid?

Which are solids?

Which are liquids?

People and Science

Icy Work!

Jean Pièrre Frémont is a sculptor.

He makes sculptures out of ice.

He begins with a huge block of ice.

Then he carves it into a shape.

When do you think his sculpture melts?

Changes

Things can change.
Shapes can change.
Colors can change.

Activity

How Does It Change?

1. Look at the liquid.
2. How does it change?
3. Look at the solid.
4. How does it change?

How did these change?

Making Pennies

Pennies are made at a mint.

Copper and other metals are used to make pennies.

The penny shapes are punched out of the metals.

An edge is pushed up around each penny.

Then the design is stamped on each side.

Chapter 1 Review

═══ What I Learned ═══

- You use your senses to find out.

- You use your 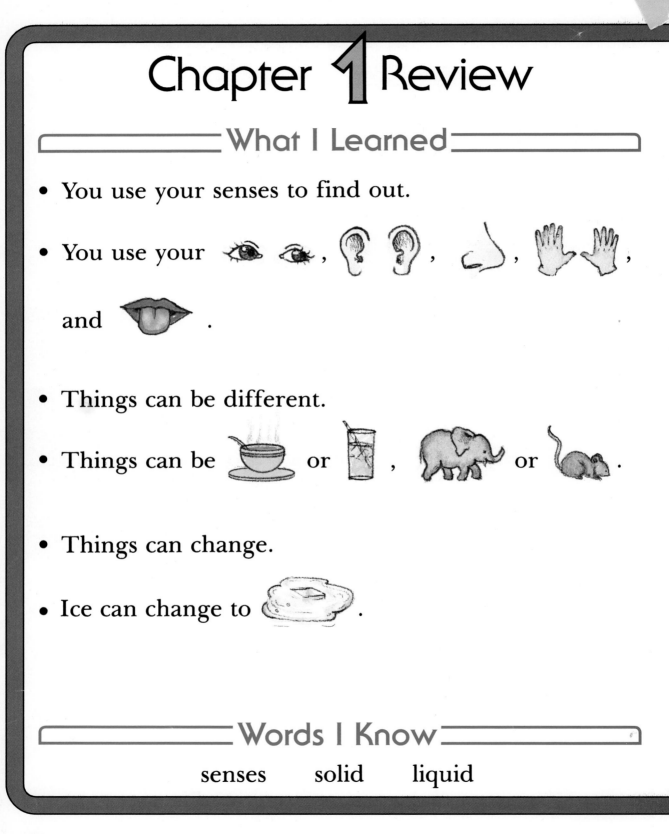 , , , ,

  and .

- Things can be different.

- Things can be or , or .

- Things can change.

- Ice can change to .

═══ Words I Know ═══

senses   solid   liquid

22

Use the pictures to answer the questions.

1. Which of these are round?
2. Which are brown?
3. Which of these would feel cold?
4. Which would feel soft?
5. Which of these are liquids?
6. Which might change to a liquid?

Books for Me

All Wet! All Wet! by James Skofield

The Look Book by Jane Belk Moncure

Take Another Look by Tana Hoban

Chapter 2

Animals

There are many kinds of animals.
How are these animals alike?
How are these animals different?

Living Things

Animals are living things.

Living things need food, water, and air.

What do animals eat?

How do animals drink?

How Are They Different?

Animals are different.

Some are big.

Some are small.

Animals have different body parts.

They use body parts to move.

How do animals move?

Animals use body parts to stay safe.

How do animals stay safe?

Animals have different body coverings.

Some body coverings keep animals safe.

What body coverings do you see?

Animals have babies.

How do baby animals look?

Activity

How Can You Group Animals?

1. Find pictures of different animals.
2. How are your animals alike?
3. How are your animals different?
4. Group your animals.

Where Animals Live

Animals live in different places.

The place an animal lives is its habitat.

Many animals live in the wild.

Wild animals have different habitats.

Where do these animals live?

Wild animals take care of themselves.

They find their own food.

They find their own homes.

Science and Technology

Like a Mother

This baby bird is being cared for at a zoo.

The zoo keeper feeds him with a puppet.

The puppet looks like the bird's mother.

Someday this bird will be set free.

It will not depend on people for food.

We care for some animals.

We care for pets.

Pets can be friends.

Where do pets live?

Activity

How Do We Care for Pets?

1. Take care of a pet for a week.
2. Make a list of what you do.
3. What did your pet eat?
4. How did you give your pet water?
5. What else did your pet need?

Here are farm animals.

What care do they need?

Why do some animals live on farms?

Some animals live in a zoo.

Who takes care of them?

Why do people go to the zoo?

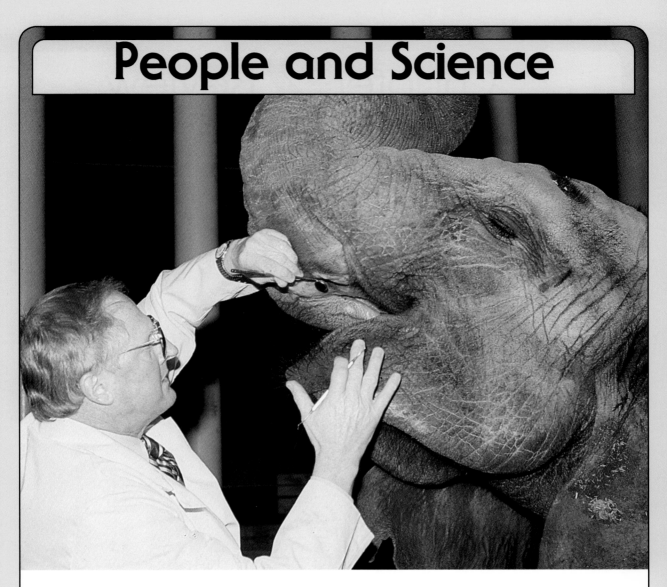

A Zoo Dentist

Dr. John Barr cares for zoo animals.

He is a zoo dentist.

Sometimes animals have sore teeth.

Dr. Barr has special tools in different sizes.

He helps animals feel better.

Chapter 2 Review

- Animals are living things.

- Living things need 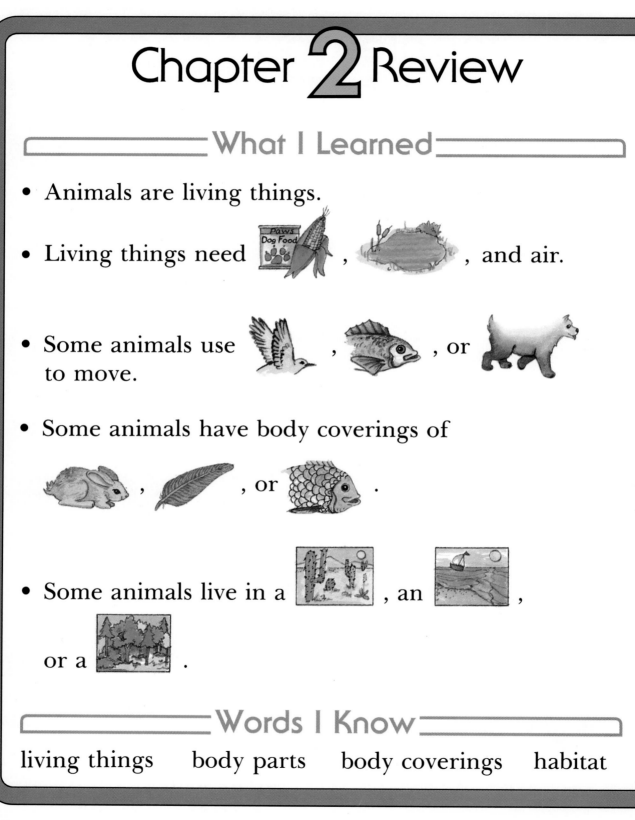 , , and air.

- Some animals use , , or to move.

- Some animals have body coverings of

  , , or .

- Some animals live in a , an ,

  or a .

Words I Know

living things   body parts   body coverings   habitat

What I Know

Use the picture to answer the questions.

1. What do living things need?
2. What ways can animals move?
3. What are body coverings?
4. What is a habitat?

Books for Me

All Kinds of Feet by Ron Goor and Nancy Goor

Is Anyone Home? by Ron Maris

A Snake Is Totally Tail Judi Barrett

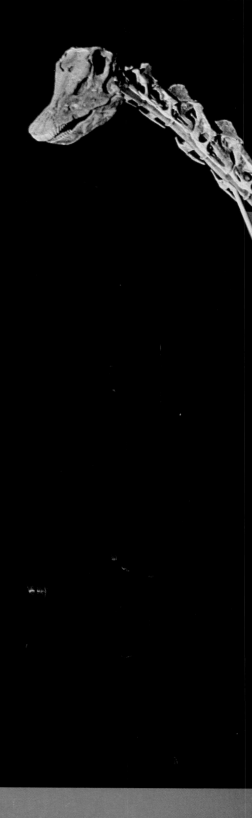

Chapter 3

Life Long Ago

What kind of animal was this?

How do you know?

COMMON JURASSIC & CRETACEOUS DINOSAURS

47

Earth Long Ago

Earth was different long ago.

It was warmer.

Some plants were different.

Some animals were different.

There were no people.

Dinosaurs

Dinosaurs lived long ago.

There were many kinds.

Some were little.

Some were very big.

Some dinosaurs ate plants.
Some ate other animals.

Which of these ate other animals?

How do you know?

Song of

1. Long a - go in steam-y swamps,
2. Bront-o-saur-us   ver-y   tall,
3. Steg - o-saur-us, fun-ny pack,
4. Tyran-no-saur-us was the King,

Some were large and ver-y slow,
Not   too smart or   ver-y   fast,
Had   two brains that you could find,
Big   as house with teeth and claws,

the Dinosaurs

Din - o saurs made heav- y stomps.
Side to side looked like a wall.
Bon - y plates all o'er his back.
Not   a - fraid of   an - y - thing.

Oth - ers quick and on the go.
Might be why he did not last.
One   in front and one be-hind.
Oth - ers were a - fraid of jaws!

Some dinosaurs lived on land.

Some lived on land and in water.

How did dinosaurs move?

Activity

What Made These Tracks?

1. Match these tracks.

2. Match these dinosaur tracks.

Dinosaurs laid eggs.

Baby dinosaurs came from eggs.

How Did It Fly?

Pterodactyls lived long ago.

Pterodactyls could fly.

People wondered how they flew.

They built a model of a pterodactyl.

They tested it in the air.

Other Animals

Other animals lived on Earth long ago.
Some lived at the same time as dinosaurs.

How did these animals move?

How Do We Know?

Dinosaurs do not live today.

People never saw them.

They died before people lived on Earth.

How do we know about animals of long ago?

We find their prints and bones in rock.

Scientists study their bones.

Activity

How Are Prints Made?

1. Roll the clay into four balls.

2. Press each ball of clay flat.

3. Push something into the clay.

4. Take it out again.

5. Look at your print with a hand lens.

Scientists guess why dinosaurs died.

They know Earth changed.

Maybe dinosaurs could not find enough food.

Chapter 3 Review

- Earth was different long ago.

- Some 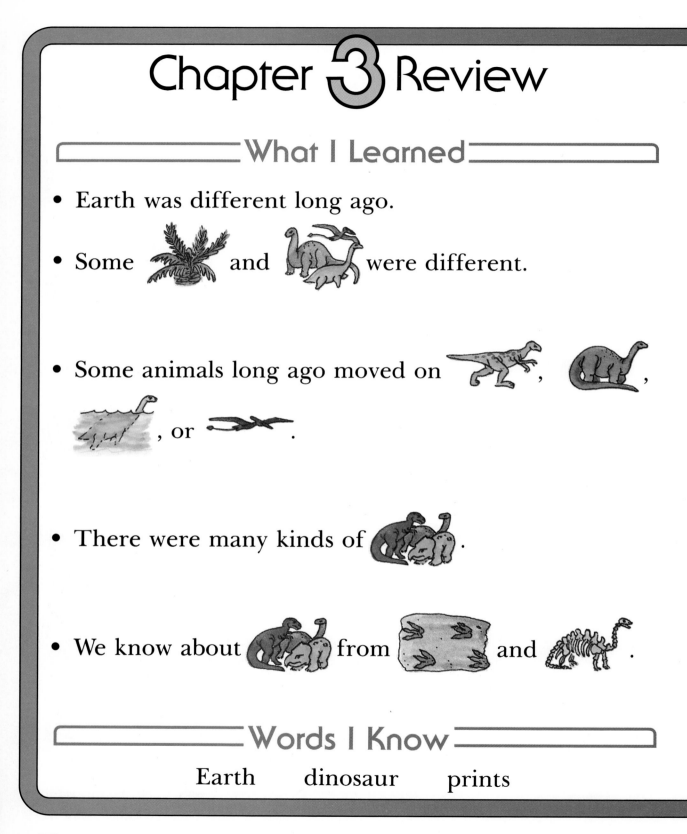 and were different.

- Some animals long ago moved on , , , or .

- There were many kinds of .

- We know about from and .

Words I Know

Earth   dinosaur   prints

What I Know

Use the picture to answer the questions.

1. What was Earth like long ago?

2. What kinds of animals lived on Earth long ago?

3. How did animals of long ago move?

4. How do we know about life long ago?

Books for Me

Baby Dinosaurs by Helen Roney Sattler

Dinosaurs from A to Z by Rosalie Davidson

My Visit to the Dinosaurs by Aliki

Chapter 4

Land Around Us

Land is all around us.

Land is made of rock and soil.

Where do you see rocks?

Rocks

There are many kinds of rocks.

Look at these rocks.

How are they different?

Activity

How Are Rocks Different?

1. Look at different rocks.
2. How can you group them?
3. Make two groups.
4. Tell about each group.

Some rocks are one color.

Some have many colors.

Minerals make rock colors.

Some minerals are shiny.

Some are dull.

Some minerals are hard.

Others are soft.

Tell about these minerals.

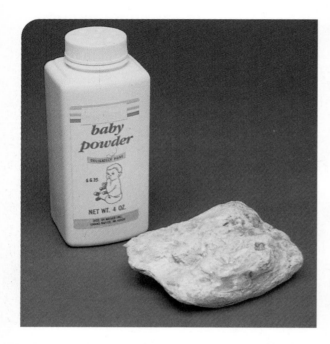

What a Gem!

Michael Mihaltian is a jeweler.

He cuts and polishes gems.

Gems are rocks or minerals.

The gems are used to make jewelry.

What gems do you like best?

Rocks Change

Most rocks are very old.

They were made before dinosaurs lived.

Some rocks are being made now.

Rocks change.

Water can change rocks.

Water can make rocks smooth.

Water can make rocks small.

Sand is made from rocks.

How does water make sand?

Activity

What Is Sand?

1. Use a hand lens to look at sand.
2. Feel the sand.
3. What do you see and feel?
4. Find ways to group pieces of sand.
5. Tell how sand is like rocks.

Soil

Soil covers much of the land.

Soil is made from rocks and minerals.

Soil has water and air.

It has dead plants and animals, too.

There are different kinds of soil.

Tell about these soils.

Plants need soil.

Soil holds air and water.

Plants use these to grow.

How do other living things use soil?

Using Land Wisely

We use rocks and minerals.

We use sand.

How do we use them?

We use land many ways.
Tell about ways we use land.

Our land is important.

We must take care of it!

Gathering Salt

We must mine for minerals like salt.

Some salt mines are underground.

Some salt is mined from the ocean.

Ocean water is gathered in pools.

Salt is left after the water evaporates.

Chapter 4 Review

- Land is all around us.

- Land is made up of 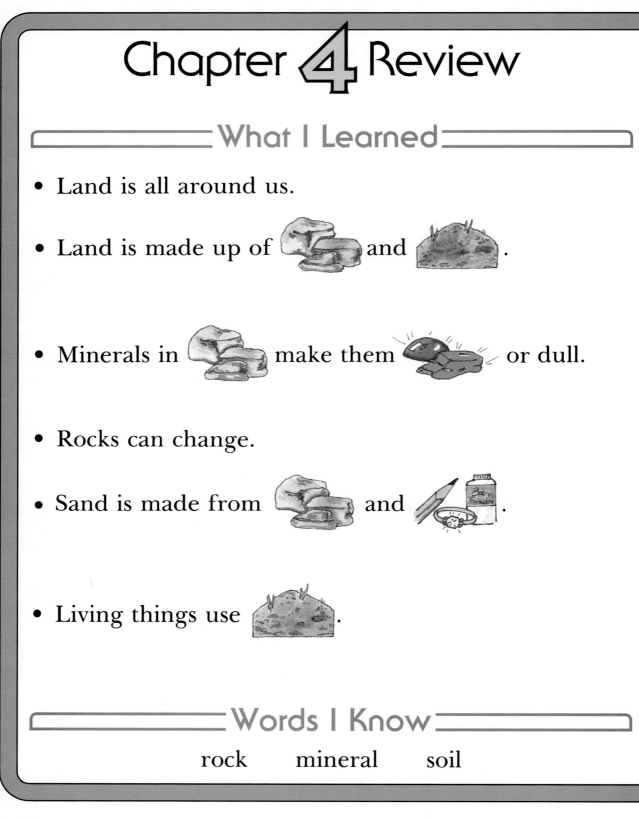 and ____.

- Minerals in ____ make them ____ or dull.

- Rocks can change.

- Sand is made from ____ and ____.

- Living things use ____.

═══ Words I Know ═══

rock   mineral   soil

Use the pictures to answer the questions.

1. Where can you find rocks?
2. How are rocks different?
3. How do rocks change?
4. How do living things use soil?

Books for Me

Mud for Sale by Brenda Nelson

The Rock Quarry Book by Michael Kehoe

Under the Ground by Eugene Booth

Chapter 5

All About You

Everyone has a body.

A body has parts.

How many parts can you name?

Your Body

Your body has many parts.

You can see some parts.

What body parts do you use to sense your world?

What parts do you use to move?

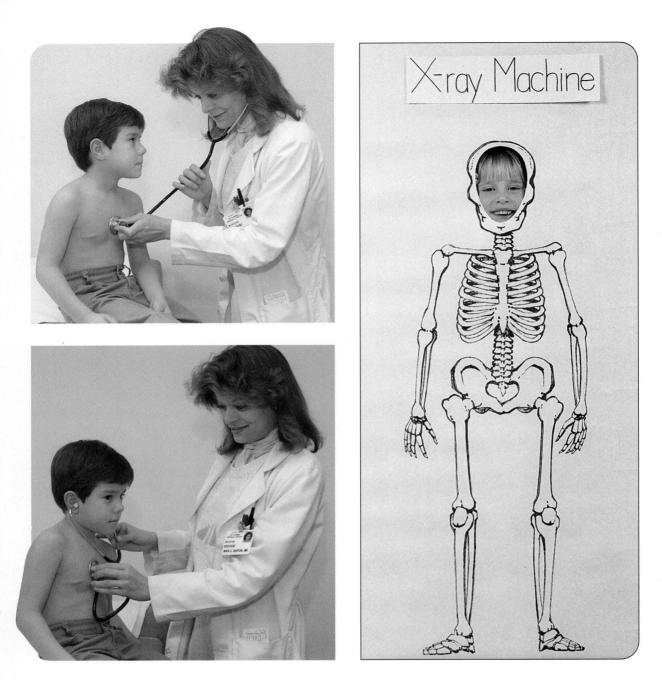

X-ray Machine

You have body parts you cannot see.

You can hear your heart.

You can feel your bones.

What other parts are inside your body?

Inside Out

What do your bones look like?

X-ray pictures show bones.

This girl has a broken arm.

The doctor took an X-ray picture of her arm.

The picture shows where the bone is broken.

Keep It Working

Your body does work.

It needs energy to work.

It needs healthful food for energy.

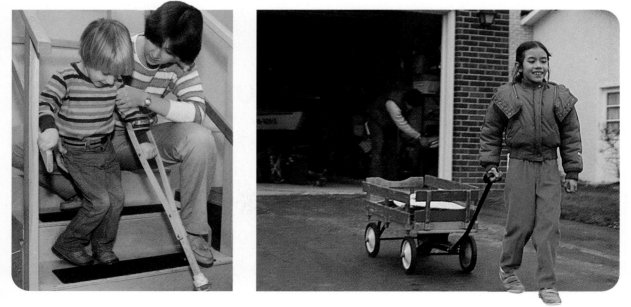

What should you eat each day?

What should you drink each day?

Some foods are not healthful.

You do not need them to help you grow.

What foods are not healthful?

Activity

What Foods Are Healthful?

1. Cut out some pictures of foods.

2. Find foods that are healthful.

3. Find foods that are not healthful.

4. Paste the foods in two groups.

Your body needs exercise.

Your heart beats faster when you exercise.

Exercise can make your heart strong.

Exercise keeps your body in good shape.

It makes you look and feel better.

Your body needs rest.

How does sleep help your body?

You need to keep your body clean.

A clean body helps you stay healthy.

Why should you keep your teeth clean?

Staying Safe

You can be safe at home.

You can be careful.

How can you stay safe?

You can stay safe going to school.

How can you stay safe on a bicycle?

How can you stay safe in a car?

Activity

How Can You Stay Safe?

1. Make a poster about being safe.
2. Tell about a safe bicycle rule.
3. Tell about a safe rule to use in a car.
4. What other rules do you follow to stay safe?

People and Science

Keeping People Safe

Juanita Peréz knows how dangerous poisons are.

She works for the Poison Control Center.

People call her if someone accidently takes poison.

Juanita tells them what to do.

She also tells them how to be safe in the future.

You Are Special

You are different from everyone else.

You are special.

Think about what you can do.

Think about what you like to do.

What is special about you?

Chapter 5 Review

What I Learned

- Your 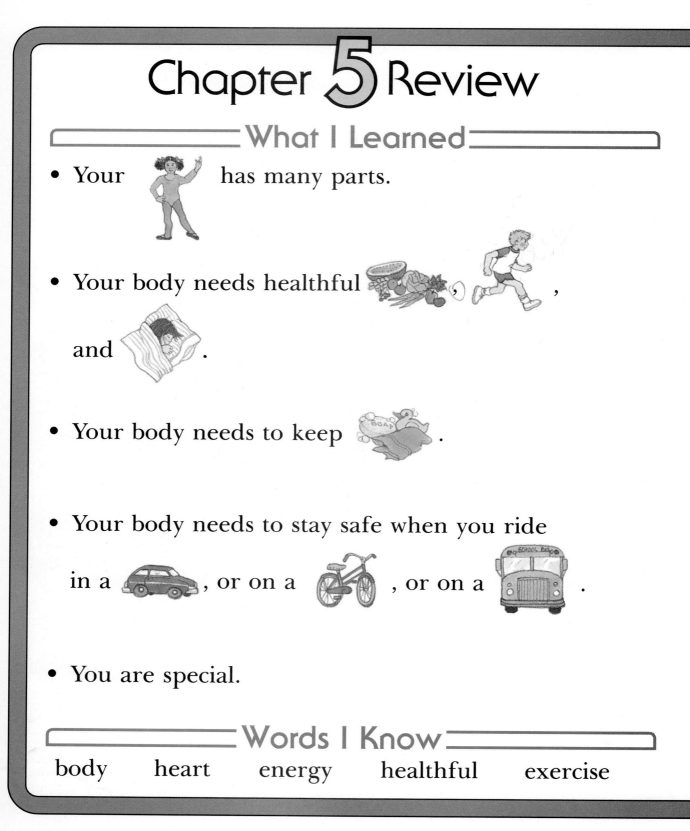 has many parts.

- Your body needs healthful , ,

  and .

- Your body needs to keep .

- Your body needs to stay safe when you ride

  in a , or on a , or on a .

- You are special.

Words I Know

body   heart   energy   healthful   exercise

What I Know

Use the picture to answer the questions.

1. What do some body parts help you to do?

2. What does your body need to stay well?

3. How can you keep your body safe?

4. What makes you special?

Books for Me

Feelings by Richard L. Allington

Jack and Jake by Aliki

My Mother Never Listens to Me by Marjorie Weinman Sharmat

Chapter 6

Earth and Space

We live on Earth.

What do you know about Earth?

What would you like to know?

Earth and the Sun

Earth has land and water.

Earth has air, too.

Where is the air?

Earth is in space.

Earth moves through space.

The sun is in space, too.
It is far away from Earth.
Which is bigger?

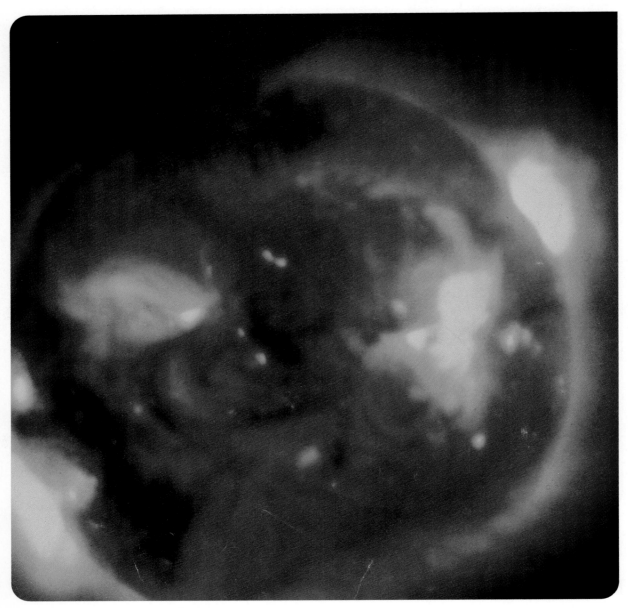

We see the sun from Earth.

Why does the sun look so small?

When the sun shines, we see shadows.

How do shadows change?

Activity

How Do Shadows Change?

1. Have a friend stand in one spot.

2. Trace your friend's shadow.

3. Do this again later in the day.

4. Measure the shadows with a string.

5. How did the shadows change?

Stars

Stars give off light.

Stars are very far away from Earth.

The sun is a star.

The sun looks bigger than other stars.

Why do you think it looks bigger?

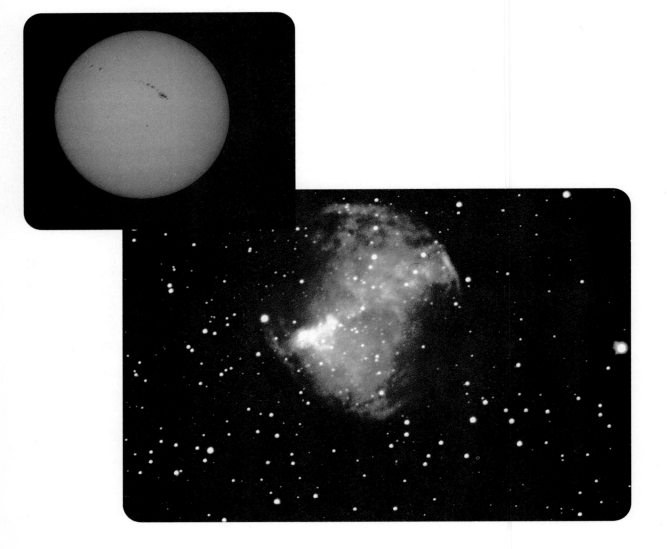

Star Gazing

Astronomers study stars.

Anita Haskins is an astronomer.

She uses a telescope to look at stars.

Some stars are farther away than the sun.

Bigger telescopes are used to find them.

People study stars.

Some stars look close to each other.

People think some stars make patterns.

Star patterns are called constellations.

Activity

What Is the Big Dipper?

1. Point the star cup at the wall.

2. Shine a light into the cup.

3. Find the star pattern on the wall.

4. What does the pattern look like?

5. Make and try your own patterns.

The Sun

The sun gives off light.

This light reaches part of Earth.

The sun seems to rise.

A new day begins.

The sun seems to set at the end of the day.

Part of Earth then has night.

What happens to the sun at night?

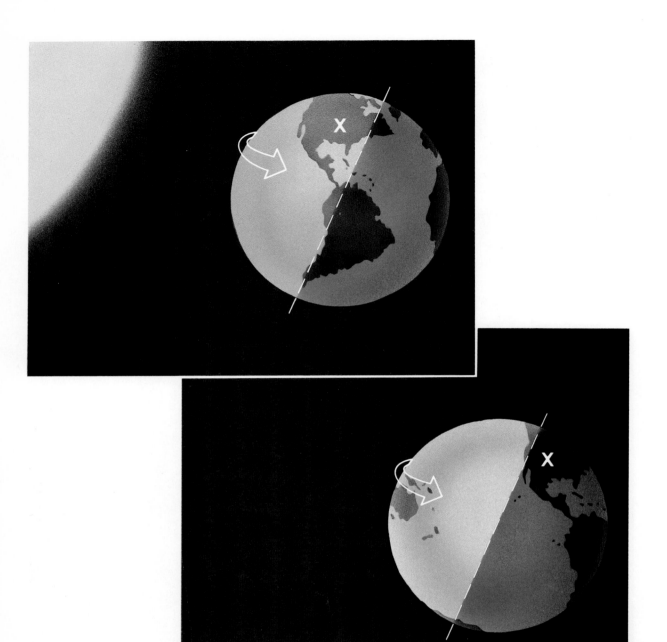

The sun does not go away.

Earth spins slowly around.

Part of Earth has day.

Another part of Earth has night.

Activity

What Makes Day and Night?

1. Suppose you are the sun.
2. Have a friend be Earth.
3. Shine light on your friend.
4. What part of your friend is day?
5. What part of your friend is night?

Space Travel

Suppose you could go into space.

You would be an astronaut.

Where would you go?

How would you get there?

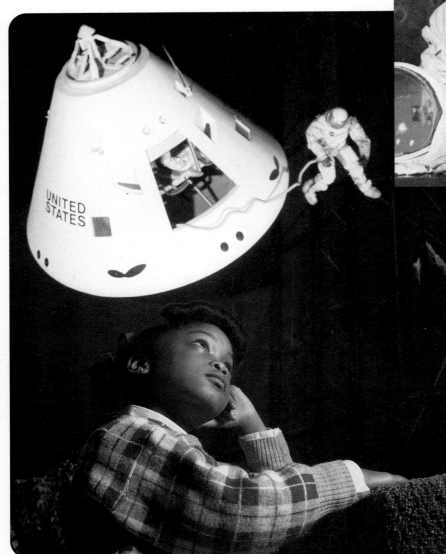

Astronauts travel in space.

They ride in special ships.

Rockets boost them into space.

Astronauts travel around Earth.

They can work in space.

Then, they come back to Earth.

What do they learn about space?

Science and Technology

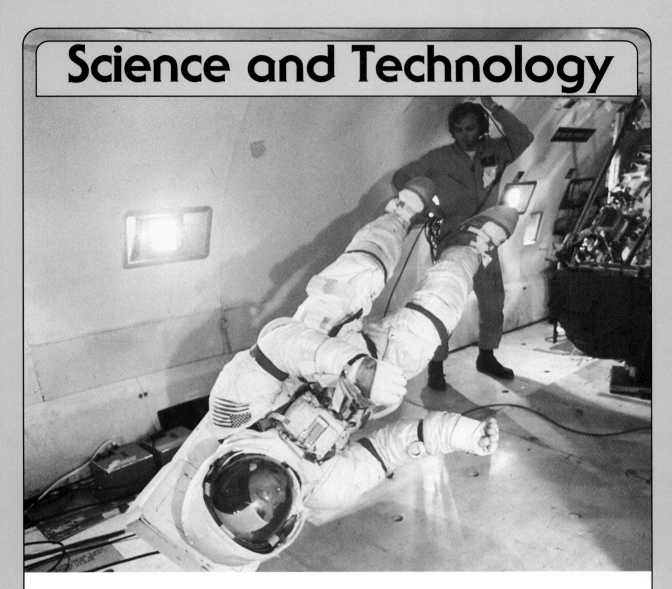

Which Way Is Up?

Astronauts travel in space.

They must be prepared.

Astronauts need to wear special suits.

They must learn to move in space.

Special suits and equipment help them learn.

Chapter 6 Review

What I Learned

- Earth moves through space.

- The 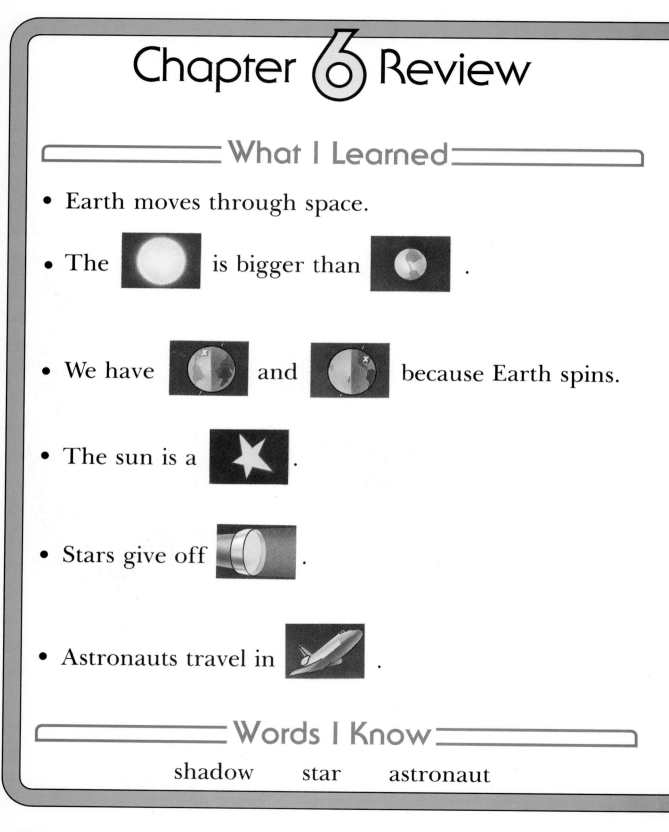 is bigger than .

- We have and because Earth spins.

- The sun is a .

- Stars give off .

- Astronauts travel in .

Words I Know

shadow   star   astronaut

Use the picture to answer the questions.

1. Why does the sun look small from Earth?

2. Why do we see shadows?

3. Why do we have day and night?

4. How could you travel in space?

Books for Me

The Miser Who Wanted the Sun by Jurg Obrist

Moon Man by Tomi Ungerer

Regards to the Man in the Moon by Ezra Jack Keats

Chapter 7

Push or Pull

Things move.

How do they move?

Why do they move?

Moving Things

You can move things.

What moves when you push?

What moves when you pull?

Sometimes it is easy to push or pull.

Sometimes it is not.

Activity

How Do You Move Things?

1. Make a list of things to move.
2. Try moving each thing.
3. Tell how you moved each one.
4. Find some easier ways to move them.
5. Try moving them now.

Things to Move	How to Move Them	Where I Moved Them	Other ways I could Move Them
1. Books	Lift		

Machines can push or pull.

Machines can do work.

Some machines have only a few parts.

Some have many parts.

How do people use machines?

Working Robots

People use robots.

Robots are machines.

Robots can do different kinds of work.

These robots help make cars.

How could a robot do work for you?

Magnets can pull.

When magnets pull, they attract.

Magnets attract some metals.

Iron is one metal magnets attract.

Activity

What Do Magnets Pull?

1. Guess what magnets will pull.
2. Make a group with these things.
3. Use a magnet.
4. Try each thing in your group.
5. What did you find out?

Some magnets have a strong pull.

Some do not.

Strong magnets pull heavy things.

People and Science

Mechanics Use Magnets

Elwin Edwards is a car mechanic.

He repairs cars that do not work.

Cars have many small metal parts.

Sometimes Elwin drops a small part onto the engine.

Then he uses a magnet to pick it up.

Magnets Push

Magnets can push.

Magnets can push each other.

When magnets push, they repel.

Magnets repel when their ends are alike.

Look at this picture.

These ends are the same.

What will he feel?

Activity

How Do the Ends of Magnets Act?

1. Use two magnets.
2. Put one end of each magnet together.
3. When do you feel a push?
4. When do you feel a pull?
5. Tell about what happens.

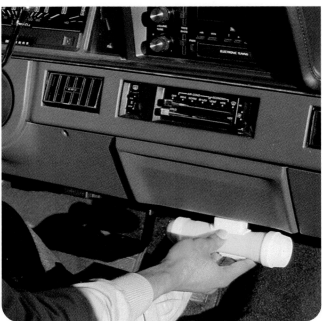

Magnets can be different sizes.

They can have different shapes.

Magnets are used many ways.

How do you use magnets?

Chapter 7 Review

What I Learned

- You can push or pull .

- Machines do work.

- Machines can or .

- Magnets can attract some .

- Magnets can repel each other.

- Magnets repel when their are alike.

Words I Know

machine   magnet   attract   repel

What I Know

Use the pictures to answer the questions.

1. How do things move?
2. How do some machines do work?
3. What can magnets pull?
4. When do magnets push?

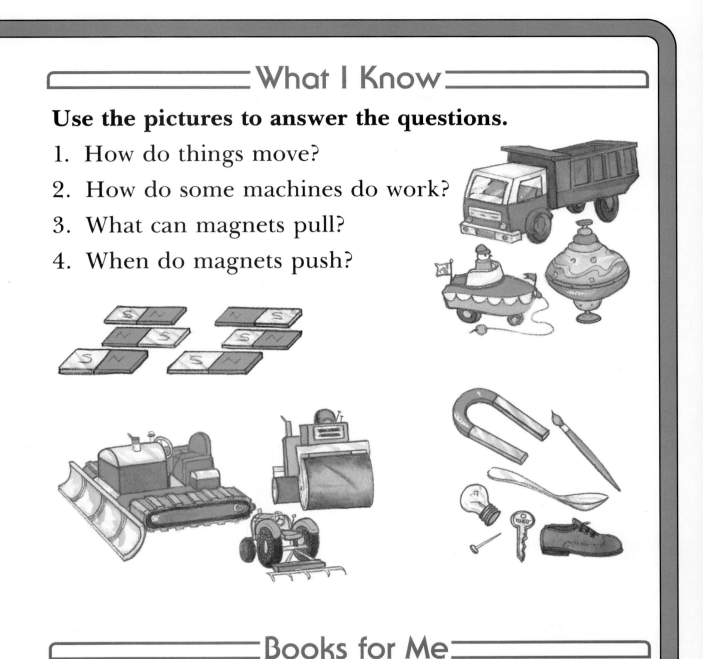

Books for Me

Look at Magnets by Rena K. Kirkpatrick

Machines by Fred Wilkin

Trucks You Can Count On by Doug Magee

Chapter 8

Plants

Plants are living things.
They use food, water, and air.
Where can you find plants?

Plant Parts

Plants have parts.

Most plants have leaves.

Most have roots and stems.

Many plants have flowers.

What plant parts do you see?

Plants use roots to take in water.

Roots also hold plants in the ground.

There are different kinds of roots.

How are these roots different?

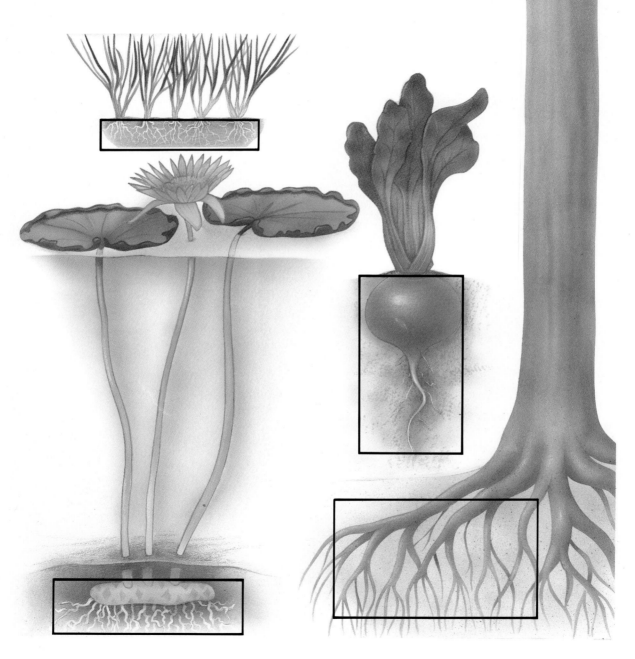

Green plants make food.

They make most food in their leaves.

Plants use this food to grow.

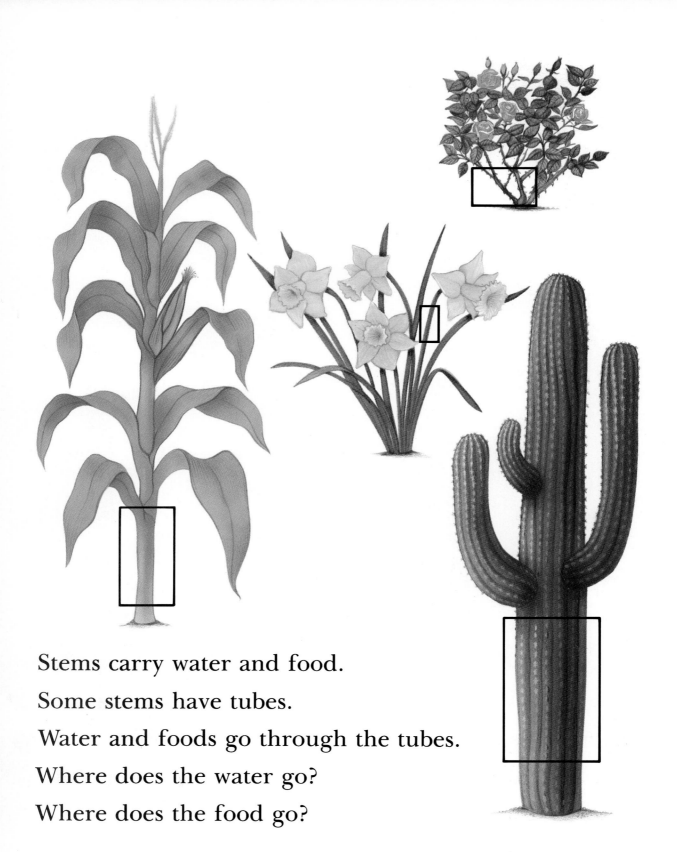

Stems carry water and food.

Some stems have tubes.

Water and foods go through the tubes.

Where does the water go?

Where does the food go?

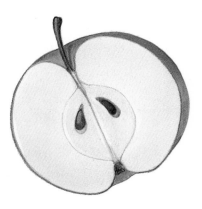

Many plants make flowers.

The flowers make seeds.

They make seeds in fruits.

What happens to some seeds?

159

Activity

How Do Seeds Grow?

1. Tape two seeds on the inside of a cup.
2. Fill the cup with soil.
3. Add water to the soil.
4. Put the cup in a warm place.
5. Draw what you see happen.

Sugaring Time

Maple syrup is made from the sap of maple trees.

The sap is collected in late winter.

A spout called a spile is tapped into a tree.

The sap drips out of the spile into a bucket.

The sap is boiled to make maple syrup.

Plants Need Animals

Some plants need animals to carry seeds.

Some seeds stick to fur.

Some seeds stick to feathers.

What happens to some of these seeds?

Flowers have pollen.

Some animals carry pollen.

Flowers need pollen to make seeds.

What animals carry pollen?

Animals Need Plants

Some animals need plants for food.

What plants do you like to eat?

Animals use plants for other things.

Some animals use trees for homes.

People use wood from trees.

How do people use wood?

How else do people use plants?

Activity

How Do Animals Use Plants?

1. Make a poster.
2. Fold your paper in half.
3. Draw plants on one side.
4. Cut pictures to show how these are used.
5. Paste them on the other side of your paper.
6. Tell about your poster.

People and Science

A Honey of a Job

Do you like honey?

Leslie Burnett does.

He raises honey bees.

The bees gather nectar from flowers.

They make honey from the nectar.

Leslie collects the honey from the beehives.

Chapter 8 Review

What I Learned

- Plants have 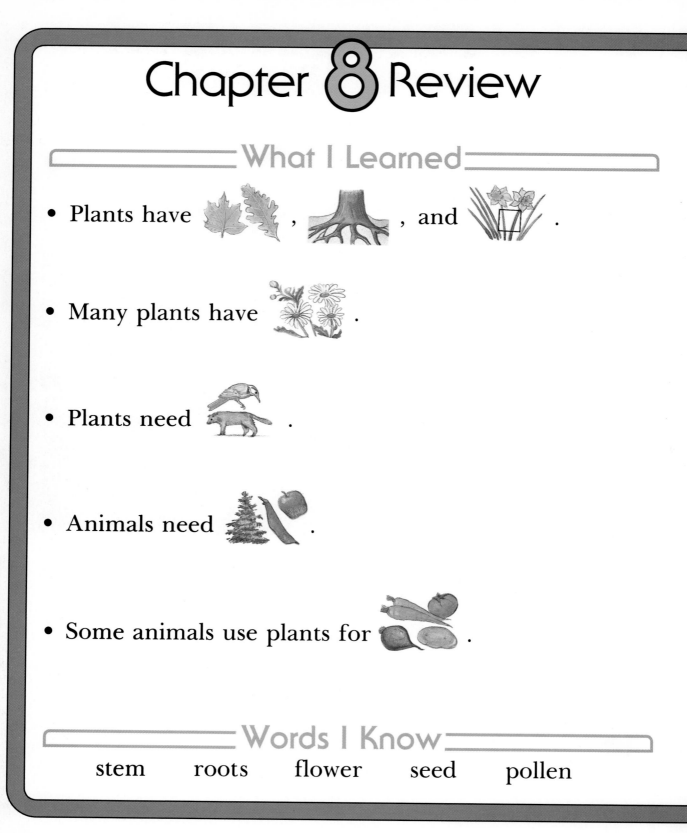 , , and .

- Many plants have .

- Plants need .

- Animals need .

- Some animals use plants for .

Words I Know

stem   roots   flower   seed   pollen

What I Know

Use the picture to answer the questions.

1. How do plants use leaves?
2. How do plants use roots?
3. Why do some plants need animals?
4. How do animals use plants?

Books for Me

A Book of Vegetables by Harriet Sobol

The Rose in My Garden by Arnold and Anita Lobel

This Year's Garden by Cynthia Rylant

Chapter 9

Water, Air, and Weather

There is a lot of water on Earth.
There is a lot of air.
Where can you find water?
Where can you find air?

Water

Water has no color.

It has no smell.

How does it taste?

What does water feel like?

How can you find out if it is heavy?

Water is a liquid.

Liquids take up space.

Look at the shape of the pool.

What is the shape of the water?

Activity

What Can You Find Out about Water?

1. Use 4 cups of water.

2. Use salt, sugar, sand, and oil.

3. Add salt to one cup and stir.

4. Tell about what you see.

5. Do steps 3 and 4 with the sugar, sand, and oil.

Sometimes water is cold.

Sometimes it is hot.

How can water change?

People and Science

People You Can Count On

Leroy Henderson is in the Coast Guard.

He serves people who live near coastal water.

Leroy likes to help rescue people.

Sometimes the Coast Guard uses a boat.

Sometimes it uses a helicopter to help people.

Air

Air is all around us.

We use air.

We cannot see air.

It is real.

Air fills up a space.

How do you know?

Air is made up of different gases.

A gas takes up space.

A gas does not have its own shape.

What gives these things a new shape?

Tell how these things changed.

How are these people using air?

Activity

What Can Air Do?

1. Make a spinner.
2. Hold it high.
3. Watch it fall.
4. What does air do?

Weather Balloons

Do balloons make you think of birthdays?

Some balloons gather weather information.

We use weather balloons to find air temperatures.

We use them to find out about wind.

Balloons can be used for fun or for work.

Weather

Air is not always the same.

Air changes.

Changes in the air make weather.

Moving air is called wind.

Sometimes weather is windy.

Weather can be warm or cool.

It can be wet or dry.

Tell about kinds of weather.

Chapter  9 Review

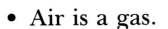 **What I Learned**

- Water is a liquid.
- It can change.
- Water has no .

- Air is a gas.
- It can fill up a space.
- A gas does not have its own .

- Changes in the air make weather.
- Weather can be  ,  , ,

  or  .

Words I Know

water   air   gas   weather   wind

What I Know

Use the pictures to answer the questions.

1. What do you know about water?
2. What do you know about air?
3. What is weather?
4. How does weather change?

Books for Me

Cloudy with a Chance of Meatballs by Judi Barrett

Rain by Peter Spier

Thunderstorm by Mary Szilagyi

Chapter 10

The Space Around You

Look at the space around you.

What is in that space?

Who takes care of it?

Your Space

Look around your desk.

Look around your classroom.

Who shares this space?

Who should take care of it?

Activity

Who Takes Care of This Space?

1. Use yarn to circle your desk.
2. List what is in this space.
3. How do you take care of it?
4. What part of this space do you share?
5. Who takes care of this?

Your space is bigger.

Everything at school is part of your space.

Who should take care of your school?

What can you do?

Our Space

Think about this park.
Who shares this space?

We share all of the space around us.
Other living things use it.

We need to care for everything around us.
What will you do?

People and Science

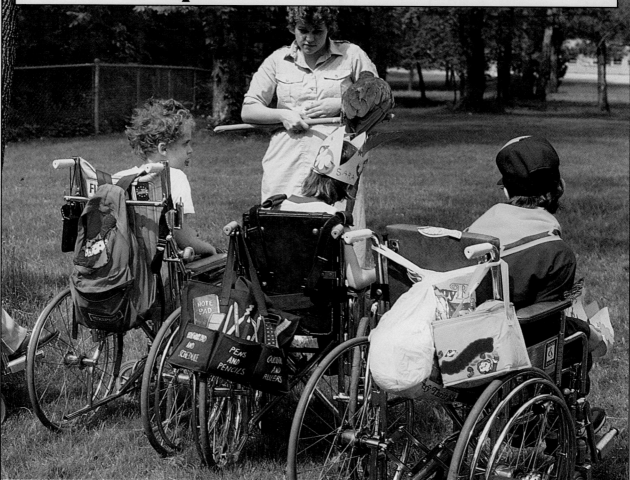

Learning to Care

Susan Snell is a park ranger.

She takes care of animals in this park.

She shares what she knows with other people.

We can learn to care for other living things.

People like Susan can help us learn.

Taking Care of Our World

We are part of the world.

Our world is big.

Everyone shares it.

What happens if people do not care for our world?

Activity

What Can I Do?

1. Go for a walk with your class.

2. What does your part of the world need?

3. What can be done?

4. Make a class list.

5. What job will you do?

At the Recycling Center

Did you ever find a new use for an old toy?

Finding new uses for things is called recycling.

Paper can be recycled.

Recycling paper can save some trees.

What are other things that can be recycled?

Chapter 10 Review

What I Learned

- Your space has your 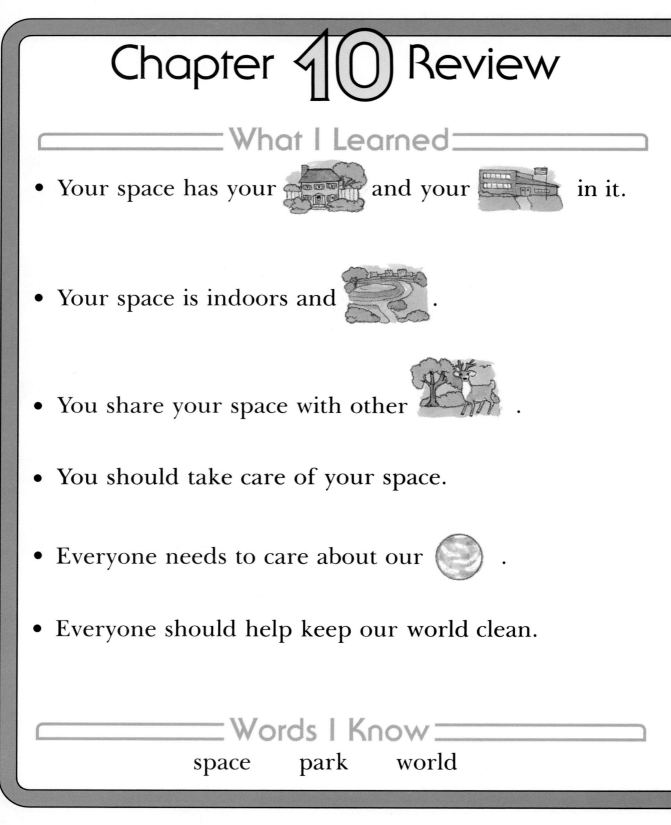 and your ▭ in it.

- Your space is indoors and ▭.

- You share your space with other ▭.

- You should take care of your space.

- Everyone needs to care about our ⬤.

- Everyone should help keep our world clean.

Words I Know

space   park   world

Use the pictures to answer the questions.

1. How do we share our space?

2. How can we care for our space?

3. Why do we need to care for our world?

4. Who should care for our world?

Books for Me

My Back Yard by Anne Rockwell

Our Garage Sale by Anne Rockwell

The Trek by Ann Jonas

Glossary

A

air

The balloon went up in the *air*.

astronaut

An *astronaut* works in space.

attract

Magnets *attract* some metal things.

B

body

The parts of your *body* work together.

body coverings

Scales are *body coverings* for fish.

body parts

Fins are *body parts* that fish use to move.

D

dinosaur

A *dinosaur* was an animal that lived long ago.

E

Earth

We live on *Earth*.

energy

We need healthful food for *energy*.

exercise

Exercise can make your body strong.

F

flower

A *flower* makes seeds in its fruit.

G
gas

A *gas* does not have its own shape.

H
habitat

A fox lives in a forest *habitat*.

healthful

Rest is *healthful* for your body.

heart

Your *heart* pumps blood.

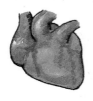

L
liquid

We can pour a *liquid*.

living things

Plants and animals are *living things*.

M

machine

A *machine* makes work easier.

magnet

A *magnet* can attract iron things.

mineral

A *mineral* can make rocks shiny or dull.

P

park

A *park* is a place for people to rest or have fun.

pollen

Bees carry *pollen* from one flower to another.

prints

We can use *prints* to learn about animals of long ago.

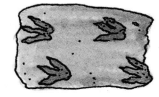

R

repel

Magnets *repel* when their ends are the same.

rock

A *rock* can be made of different kinds of minerals.

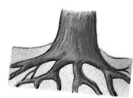

roots

Plants get water through their *roots*.

S

seed

A *seed* can grow into a new plant.

senses

We use our *senses* to find out about our world.

shadow

We can see our *shadow* on a sunny day.

soil

Soil is made from rocks and minerals.

solid

A *solid* has a shape.

space

The sun and the other stars are out in *space*.

Your *space* is what is around you.

star

A *star* gives off light.

stem

A *stem* is a part of a plant.

W

water

Water has no color or smell.

weather

Weather can be cloudy, sunny, rainy, or snowy.

wind

Wind is moving air.

world

We should take care of our *world*.

Index

PHOTO CREDITS
COVER: Breck P. Kent